Discovering

OTTERS

Martin Banks

The Bookwright Press
New York · 1988

Discovering Nature

Further titles are in preparation

Cover *This Eurasian otter has just come out of the water. Its wet, spiky fur will look woolly when dry.*

Frontispiece *A pair of North American otters surface to survey their surroundings.*

First published in the
United States in 1988 by
The Bookwright Press
387 Park Avenue South
New York, NY 10016

Library of Congress Cataloging-in-Publication Data

Banks, Martin, 1936–
    Discovering otters / Martin Banks.
        p. cm. — (Discovering nature)
    Bibliography: p.
    Includes index.
    Summary: An introduction to the physical characteristics, habits, and natural environment of both the sea and freshwater otter. Also discusses the different types found around the world and what is being done to assure their survival.
    ISBN 0–531–18227–4
    1. Otters — Juvenile literature. (1. Otters.) I. Title. II. Series.
QL737.C25B285 1988   88–5954
599.74′447 — dc19   CIP
                                       AC

First published in 1988 by
Wayland (Publishers) Limited
61 Western Road, Hove
East Sussex BN3 1JD, England

© Copyright 1988 Wayland (Publishers) Limited
All rights reserved

Typeset by DP Press Ltd., Sevenoaks, Kent
Printed in Italy by Sagdos S.p.A., Milan

Contents

1
Introducing Otters

The Asian short-clawed otter is the smallest otter in the world.

What are Otters?

Otters are members of the family of animals called **mustelids**. It includes badgers, weasels, pine martens and polecats. All of them have scent glands at the base of the tail, which the animals use to emit a powerful smell. Otters are **amphibious** creatures, well adapted to a life in water or on land. They are powerful swimmers, both at the surface and underwater. But because they are air-breathing **mammals**, they must come to the surface regularly to breathe. Although otters are at home in water, they also come on land to dry their fur, to feed and to rest.

Otters are found in many countries. There are over a dozen different **species**. Although they usually live in freshwater lakes and rivers, some otters are found on seacoasts too. One species, the sea otter, lives only in the

sea along the Pacific coast of North America.

Otters vary in size from the short-clawed otter of Asia, which is about 90 cm (3 ft) long and weighs about 5 kg (11 lb), to the South American giant

Three South American giant otters rest on a tree trunk in the jungle of Peru.

otter, which can be 1.8 meters (6 ft) long, and weigh 30 kg (66 lb). Sea otters weigh more, up to 45 kg (99 lb).

The Body of an Otter

Despite the differences in size, all types of otters have a similar shape. A long, heavy body, a small head and a thick, tapering tail are the most distinctive features. The front and hind legs are short, and there is no obvious neck. All these features give an otter a very streamlined appearance and help it to move easily in water. In addition, several species have partially webbed feet.

An otter has small ears, a wide, blunt muzzle with prominent whiskers and small, beady eyes. Otters are **carnivores**. They have sharp, strong teeth for holding and tearing their **prey**. Most species feed on fish and other **aquatic** animals.

A pair of Eurasian otters. All otters have a similar streamlined shape that helps them move easily in water.

An otter has small ears and eyes, long, sensitive whiskers and strong, sharp teeth. This is a clawless otter.

A pair of spotted-necked otters. Notice their fully webbed feet.

On land, otters have a humped appearance. The long body is arched upward over short, sturdy legs. The heavy tail lies flat behind it. Most otters have brownish colored fur. It consists of a soft, dense undercoat and longer guard hairs, which help to trap air when the animal is in the water.

This helps to keep it from becoming waterlogged.

Some species have distinct markings, such as pale fur on the throat and underside of the body. The spotted-necked otter of Africa has a pale throat spotted with darker patches. When wet, an otter's fur looks darker, often almost black.

Otter or Mink?

A mink with its prey. People often confuse mink and otters.

In North America and Europe, otters are often found sharing their **habitat** with another, smaller member of the mustelid family, the mink. Mink and otters are frequently confused, although it is only their general shape that is at all similar. Mink are considerably smaller than the otters that live in the same countries. They are usually black all over with a white spot under the chin, although other color varieties exist. Otters are dark colored above and usually lighter below. An otter is longer and heavier than a mink. A mink has a small, pointed head and short bushy tail in comparison with an otter. Although mink are often seen swimming, they are less aquatic than otters. They do not have webbing between the toes like an otter, and are not such strong or graceful swimmers.

You may see a mink hunting in or alongside a river in daylight. They are bold creatures and have little fear of people, unlike the more retiring otter. Many people confuse the two species, thinking they have seen an otter when they have really seen a mink.

pointed head

bushy tail

MINK

long whiskers

smaller than the otter

thick tapering tail

OTTER

webbed feet

pale throat

2
Where Otters Live

The North American river otter spends a lot of time in the water hunting for fish.

Rivers, Streams and Oceans

All otters spend some of their time in the water. The Eurasian otter lives in a particularly wide variety of habitats. In Britain and Europe it is found in lakes and marshes, along rivers and streams and, sometimes, along the seacoast. The short-clawed otter of Asia lives in rice-paddy fields and marshes. The smooth otter, which is found in the same continent, prefers slow-flowing rivers and mangrove swamps. In both North and South America there are different otters, which live in rivers and in the ocean.

The amount of time otters spend in the water varies. The little short-clawed otters spend their time hunting for food in marshes and shallow dikes. They are **terrestrial** for much of the time. But the sea otter of North America stays afloat almost all its life and hardly ever comes

Above *Sea otters live in the ocean, rarely coming ashore. They rest and sleep afloat among the kelp.*

Right *A common otter about to enter a partly frozen river. Its thick coat helps to keep it warm in winter.*

ashore. In between are several other kinds of otters, which spend part of their time hunting and traveling in the water and the remainder on land.

Banks and Shore Lines

Although otters are water-loving creatures, most of them spend some of their time on dry land. They were originally land animals, and even now they still need to come ashore to dry their fur and groom themselves.

When an otter catches a large fish, it usually brings it to the bank before eating it.

Despite having a long body and

These Indian smooth-coated otters have worn away the grass, forming a path to the water's edge.

This otter has just come out of the water. Otters usually groom themselves and rest on land.

Quiet stretches of Scottish coast are often inhabited by otters. They make their dens among the rocks.

heavy tail, which are well designed for swimming, otters can move easily on land too. The Eurasian otter often travels overland, and it may make journeys of over a mile away from water. When otters travel on land, they flatten the vegetation as they pass by. Where they use the same routes frequently, regular pathways are formed. You can sometimes find these alongside rivers where otters are living.

Dens and Lairs

Most species of otters spend the hours of daylight resting in a den or lair. This is always out of the water, but usually close to it. Eurasian otters often use the natural hollows under the roots of trees growing beside the water. In places where there are no trees, an otter will use a hole in the bank or under some rocks. In its den the otter is warm and dry and safe from disturbance. Often the entrance is underwater. This means that the otter can enter and leave without being seen. An otter's lair or den may sometimes be lined with grass or rushes, especially when a female otter has young.

Otters also rest aboveground, in

South American giant otters entering their den. Their wide, flat tails help them steer in the water.

Otters often make their dens in the hollows under the roots of trees. This is a river otter in South Carolina.

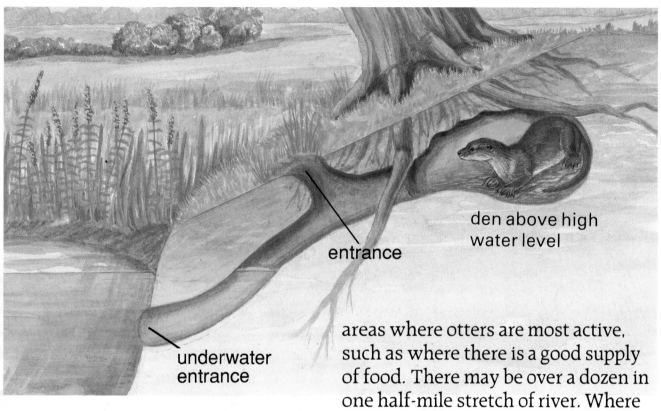

entrance

den above high
water level

underwater
entrance

reeds or among thick vegetation.
Sometimes an otter has more than
one den or lair in the area in which it
lives. As it travels around its
territory, it uses these places as
temporary homes.

There are likely to be more dens in
areas where otters are most active,
such as where there is a good supply
of food. There may be over a dozen in
one half-mile stretch of river. Where
an otter's lair is well used, there will
often be a very obvious path leading
into the lair. There may also be
droppings left near the entrance.
These are sure signs that otters are
using the den frequently and perhaps
even **breeding** in it.

3
How Otters Live

The Eurasian otter lives alone for most of the year.

A Solitary Existence

Some otters are **solitary** animals. They live alone except when a male and female come together to breed. The Eurasian otter is one such species. After the **cubs** leave their mother when they are several months old, they live on their own for much of the time.

Despite this way of life, otters keep in touch with one another by using signals. Most important is scent, produced by the **glands** under the tail. These glands produce a strong, musky-smelling substance, and otters' droppings carry a similar smell.

Otters leave their droppings on boulders in streams, on fallen logs, under bridges and in other places in their territories. They also scrape together loose soil or tufts of grass, and deposit scent on them. These are called "sign heaps." Other otters

This heap of Eurasian otter droppings is a form of sign language to other otters.

passing the same way will find these places. From the scent they carry, they learn about the other otters living in the area. Scent may help an otter discover whether there is a female ready for breeding or perhaps a rival male in the area. The scent otters leave is a form of sign language.

Living in Groups and Pairs

Several species of otters are **sociable** animals. They live in pairs or family groups all year 'round. The males of these kinds of otters help to rear the young, although in the giant and smooth-coated species, it is actually the female of a pair that is the **dominant** animal. Social otters travel,

South American giant otters live in family groups – they are sociable animals.

hunt and rest together in a group. In order to help them keep together, the otters have a variety of high-pitched twittering calls, which they use to keep in contact, especially when swimming or searching for food.

These otters also leave scent and

droppings at special places along the water's edge. They mix and trample the soil as a way of advertising that this is part of the territory of one particular family. The giant otter of South America clears areas up to 8 square meters (85 sq ft) along the river banks. These places become quite bare and smell strongly of the otters that make them.

Sea otters live in much larger groups. They are the only otters that may be found in gatherings of several hundred. It seems that these otters are drawn together by the supplies of their favorite foods, rather than because they are social.

Colonies of sea otters live where there is a plentiful supply of shellfish.

In the Water

Otters are well adapted to an aquatic lifestyle. Only the Oriental short-clawed otter and the African clawless otter rarely enter deep water. Their feet are less webbed than other species.

The long, muscular body, streamlined shape and heavy tail all combine to make the otter a good swimmer. At the surface, an otter swims by using a paddling motion of the feet, something like a dog. The strong tail, often called the rudder, provides balance and steering. When

Sea otters are completely aquatic and do not need to come ashore to rest or to groom. Their back legs are like powerful flippers.

The long, slim shape of the otter helps it glide easily through the water.

an otter dives underwater, the front feet are held against the body. The otter swims using powerful kicks of the hind feet, combined with muscular movements of its hind end and tail. This gives it greater speed for catching prey or escaping danger.

When swimming underwater, an otter closes its ear openings and **nostrils**. Its eyes remain open. It can stay underwater for a few minutes. Then it must return to the surface for air. An otter's fur is not **waterproof**. Air trapped among the hair helps to **insulate** it while swimming. But if it stayed in the water too long, an otter would eventually become water-logged and drown.

Moving on Land

When an otter first comes out of the water, its coat has a spiky appearance. That is because the longer guard hairs stick together. To squeeze the water out of its coat, an otter will roll on the ground and rub itself against solid

objects like stones. As the fur dries, it becomes woolly-looking.

Most otters are **nocturnal**, spending the daytime resting. During the night they move around on land as well as in the water. A period of hunting and swimming is usually followed by the otter's coming ashore to dry itself, groom its fur and rest.

Otters are often thought of as being very playful creatures. Places have been found where it is obvious that otters have repeatedly slid down a river bank into the water. But this may simply be a well-used trail, where an otter path enters the water, and not a place where the animals come together to spend time playing. Wild otters, like most other animals, probably do most of their playing

A river otter in Florida rests on the trunk of a palm tree. When it is wet, its coat looks spiky.

when they are very young.

Out of the water, otters move with a waddling walk. The body is arched upward, and held well clear of the ground. The tail may drag along the ground or be held in a slightly raised position. At a faster speed, otters can move at a bounding gallop. When moving on land, otters often pause to look around. Some species stand on their hind legs in order to get a better view, but drop to all fours when they start moving again.

Above *On land, some kinds of otters stand on their back legs to look around.*

Right *This snow slide into the water was made by an otter.*

4
Food and Feeding

Most otters eat aquatic creatures such as fish, crabs and frogs. This river otter is eating a fish.

What Otters Eat

Otters are carnivorous animals. Because they live in and close to water, they feed chiefly on fish and other aquatic creatures like crabs and frogs. They also eat small mammals and birds, particularly those found near water, like ducks. Other types of prey may be eaten at certain times of the year, but in smaller amounts.

The Eurasian otter has a varied **diet**. In Britain it is known to eat many different kinds of freshwater fish, particularly slow-moving ones like roach, perch and bream and small ones like minnows and sticklebacks. Along seacoasts, large numbers of crabs and saltwater fish are eaten. Eels are a particular favorite.

In spring and summer, otters may eat frogs and young water birds. Salmon and trout are sometimes caught, but otters cannot really be

blamed for stealing a fisherman's catch. Scientists have been able to identify exactly what otters eat by examining their droppings, which contain the remains of their recent meals. Fish remains show up in the form of small bones and scales in the droppings. These and other animal

A sea otter feeding on a sea urchin.

remains can be identified to prove exactly what an otter has been eating.

The North American sea otter has a rather different diet. Its favorite foods are shellfish, especially mussels and a type of clam called an abalone.

Catching Their Food

Otters catch their food in one of two ways. Most otters chase their prey and grasp it with their teeth and jaws. But the two smallest kinds of otters, from Asia and Africa, use another method. These otters have well-developed toes on their front feet, more like those of a monkey. Using these toes like fingers, the otters dig for their food, mainly crabs and frogs, in shallow water. They catch their food with their "hands."

Other otters dive underwater when hunting prey. They use their eyes to find and follow fish, but in murky water or dim light they may rely on the sensitive whiskers on their faces, to help them detect food. To catch a fish, an otter swims at its fastest speed, hoping to tire out its prey or catch it unaware. To catch eels, flatfish, crabs and other creatures that

The Asian short-clawed otter catches food using the well-developed "fingers" on its front feet.

live on the bottom, the otter has to search under rocks and stones.

Once it has caught something, an otter will carry it to the surface. Small prey may be eaten afloat, but usually larger catches are taken ashore. If the catch is slippery, like an eel, the otter grips it with its forepaws while eating. Afterward, the otter will clean itself, especially if it has eaten a slippery eel.

Because otters have very rapid **digestion**, they have to eat frequently. In the course of one night's

Right *Sea otters often use a rock to crack open clams and other shellfish.*

Below *When an otter catches a large fish it brings it ashore before eating it.*

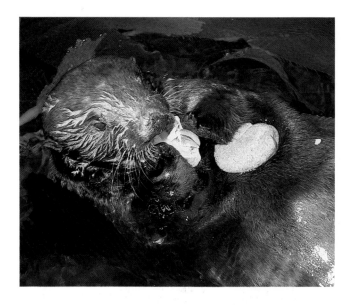

activity, an otter may have several feeding sessions. An adult Eurasian otter needs about 1 kg (2 lb) of food per day to keep in good condition.

Unlike other otters, sea otters rarely chase fish. They feed mostly on shellfish, which they collect from the seabed. Returning to the surface, a sea otter floats on its back, holding its food with its front paws. Sea otters sometimes use heavy rocks to remove and smash open their abolones.

5
Family Life

It is easy for sea otters to find mates because they live in large groups.

Finding a Mate

Some otters live on their own for most of the year. During their travels along waterways, they leave scent and droppings where other otters will find them. This is usually how a male otter discovers there is a female nearby. If the scent of a female shows that she is ready to breed, the male otter will look for her. Otters also communicate by voice. The Eurasian otter has a high-pitched squeak or whistle, which is its contact call. Other growling and sighing noises are used if an otter is angry or afraid.

Otters that live in family groups or pairs have no need to search for mates. If the otters are living in a family group, the males may fight over a female. In solitary species, too, more than one male may be attracted to the same female. Usually the strongest male becomes her mate.

A North American river otter calls out to contact other otters in the area.

both on land and in the water, for several hours before mating takes place. This allows the two animals to become better known to each other. Otters that live together all year 'round already know each other, so there is less need for long chasing and playing sessions.

Because the sea otter lives in **colonies**, there is a wide selection of mates to choose from. It appears that male sea otters have territories close to those of large groups of females with young. Female sea otters looking for a mate simply swim into the territory of a nearby male.

Otters usually mate in the water. Often the pair will chase and play,

When a solitary species of otter finds a mate, they play together for several hours before mating.

Baby Otters

The usual **gestation** period of an otter is about nine weeks. But the American river otter, and the sea otter, both take much longer than this. The young may be born twelve months after mating. That is because the fertilized eggs of the female do not start developing immediately. Weasels and badgers, which are also mustelids, share this method, and so do some deer and seals.

When a female otter is ready to give birth, she goes in search of a secluded den. Usually this is in a side stream or other quiet stretch of water. She may line the chamber with grass or reeds before the **cubs** are born. From one to six cubs are born in a litter. Two is the usual number for most otters, but sea otters never have more than one cub

A baby sea otter sucking milk from its mother. Sea otters are born in the water, on a bed of floating seaweed.

at a time.

    The cubs are blind and helpless at birth, with short, soft fur. For the first few days, the mother remains with them all the time, providing the cubs

A Eurasian otter plays with her cubs.

with milk and warmth. Soon, she begins to leave them for intervals while she hunts for food.

Growing Up

For the first three months, the cubs rely on their mother for food, warmth and protection. When their eyes open, they begin to explore their surroundings. Later on, they begin to move about outside the den. But otter cubs are not natural swimmers. Only

Baby sea otters ride on their mother's chest, but they must learn to swim at an early age.

the sea otter, which is usually born in the water and rides on its mother's chest while she swims on her back, knows how to swim at an early age. Otters were originally land animals.

Even now, the cubs must learn how to swim. Usually the mother lures them into the water, but sometimes she may have to pull them in. Once they can swim, the cubs begin to chase fish, learning to hunt for themselves.

Young otters learn how to hunt and take care of themselves by playing together.

After several months the cubs gradually become independent. When they are about eighteen months old, they will themselves be able to breed.

The Eurasian otter is unusual among mammals of Northern regions. It has no set time for breeding, and may produce cubs in almost any month of the year.

6
Enemies and Survival

Humans are the worst enemies of the otter. This river otter died as a result of being caught in a trap.

Otters and People

People are the only real enemies of otters. In the past, otters have been hunted for their fine skins, called pelts. These were made into clothes for people to wear. The sea otter was hunted so much it nearly became **extinct**. Now it is protected, and its numbers have increased again. But other species, like the South American giant otter, are still very rare.

In Britain, otters used to be treated as pests. They were trapped and killed wherever possible, because it was believed they ate large quantities of valuable salmon and trout. We now know that this is not true.

Otters were also hunted for sport. A pack of hounds was used to find an otter and then to follow its scent until the otter was caught and killed. Now it is illegal to catch or kill an otter in most parts of Britain. Free from this kind of persecution, otters have a better chance of increasing their numbers again.

In recent years, a number of accounts have been written by people who have kept otters as pets. They all agree that otters are delightful and entertaining creatures and, in

South American giant otters are very rare. If people left them alone they would have a chance to increase their numbers.

captivity are extremely playful. But the otter has another side to its nature. It can be savage and inflict serious wounds with its sharp teeth if it becomes angry or frightened. Pet otters need expert attention, with plenty of space, both land and water, and the right things to eat.

The sea otter is now a protected animal – it is against the law to kill one.

Draining and Polluting

Because they are at the top of a **food chain**, otters have few, if any, natural enemies. But in recent years, otters have become very rare in some parts of the world. One of the main reasons for this is that their habitats have been spoiled by humans. Otters need marshes, rivers and lakes to live in. Many of these places are being drained to provide more land to build on and for farming. It means there are fewer suitable places for otters to live.

In many areas, the thick growth of trees and waterside plants near rivers have been cut down. Otters use these places to rest and rear their young. When the banks of a river are cleared and the trees cut down, otters will soon move away.

Besides clearing and draining wetlands, people have sprayed **pesticides** on the land. These kill weeds and pests and improve the land for farming, but pesticides often contain chemical substances that are poisonous to other animals too. When rain washes these chemicals into the rivers and streams, fish and other aquatic animals suffer badly. If otters eat a lot of poisoned fish, some of the poison enters their own bodies. It may not be enough poison to kill or injure the otters but often it is enough to prevent them from breeding

The disturbance of wetland, directly affects otters because it destroys their habitat.

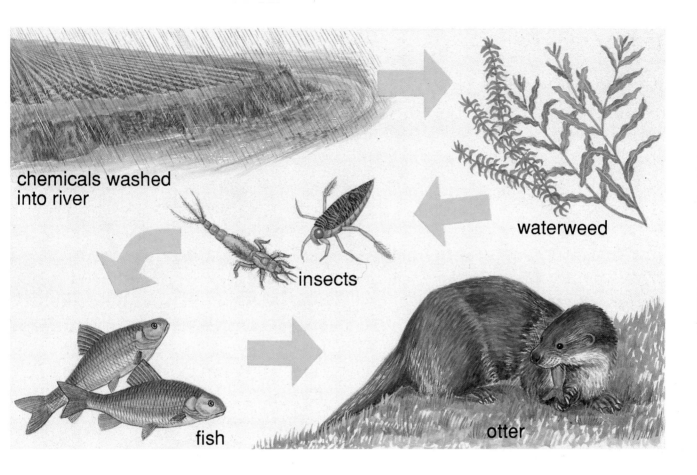

chemicals washed into river

insects

waterweed

fish

otter

successfully. If many otters stop breeding for a number of years, the population will begin to decline.

Pollution and disturbance of waterways are two of the reasons why

A disaster chain showing how chemicals sprayed on crops eventually affects otters.

otters have become so scarce in some countries in recent years.

7
Looking for Otters

If you find a well-worn track leading to water, you may be lucky enough to see an otter using it.

Otters usually emerge from their resting places at dusk or after dark. It is very difficult to watch them in the wild. They are shy creatures with good senses of smell and hearing. If you happen to be close to an otter, it is likely to sense you first. It will quickly hide in the vegetation or dive below the surface of the water.

There are some places where you have a better chance of seeing otters. The sea otter can be seen off the coasts of Alaska and California, feeding among the beds of **kelp** in which it lives. On the coasts of Scotland, otters are often active by day, but you still need time and patience, along with plenty of luck, to see them.

Perhaps the best chance of seeing otters is to take up fishing. Long hours of sitting by a river bank may bring its reward, a fleeting glimpse in the dusk of a sleek animal swimming in the water or wandering along the bank.

Even if otters are very difficult to observe, you can search for their tracks and droppings along the banks of rivers and streams. These signs will tell you if otters are present. The five-toed tracks show clearly in mud, and may lead into and out of the water. Look for blackish droppings containing fish bones and scales; look under bridges and on banks and large boulders in streams.

Remember that otters do not like being disturbed. It is better to leave anything that looks like a den or lair well alone. Even the scent of a human may be enough to make the otter abandon its home and move away.

It is difficult to see otters in the wild but you can see signs of their presence such as tracks in the mud and droppings.

Glossary

Amphibious Living both on land and in water.

Aquatic Living on or in the water only.

Breeding Producing and rearing young.

Carnivores Animals that eat meat or flesh.

Colonies Large numbers of animals living together or coming together to breed.

Cubs The word for baby otters.

Diet The food that an animal eats.

Digestion The process of breaking down food in the stomach and intestines.

Dominant Being stronger than others and thus able to be leader.

Extinct Having died out completely.

Food Chain The relationship between animals that feed on other animals. Example: a worm is eaten by a shrew, which is eaten by a hawk, which is eaten by a fox. The worm is at the bottom of the chain and the fox is at the top.

Gestation The period between mating and birth, when the young develop inside their mother's body.

Glands Parts of the body that produce a special substance, such as musk or scent.

Habitat The type of place in which an animal species normally lives.

Insulate To keep warm and dry.

Kelp A species of seaweed, found growing along rocky coasts.

Mammals Warm-blooded animals with hair or fur on the body. Human beings are mammals.

Mustelids A group of animals with glands at the base of the tail that give off a strong scent.

Nocturnal Active at night.

Nostrils Openings in the nose used for breathing.

Pesticides Poisonous chemicals that are used to kill pests.

Pollution Poisoning of the atmosphere, land or water with pesticides or other man-made impurities, such as factory smoke and industrial waste.

Prey An animal that is killed and eaten by another animal.

Sociable Living in pairs or groups and enjoying the company of others.

Solitary Living alone.

Species Animals or plants of one particular

kind.
Temporary For only a short time.
Terrestrial Living on land.
Territory A clearly defined area where an animal lives and which it usually defends against others.
Waterproof Providing complete protection from water.

Finding Out More

The following books will tell you more about otters:

Otters by Noel Simon. Biblio Distribution Centre, 1985.
Otters, Skunks and Their Family by Dorothy H. Patent. Holiday House, Inc., 1973.
Ring of Bright Water by Gavin Maxwell. E.P. Dutton, 1965.
Sea Otter by Julian May. Creative Education, Inc., 1972.
Sea Otters by Evelyn Shaw. Harcourt Brace Jovanovich, Inc., 1980.
Sea Otters and Seaweed by Patricia Lauber. Garrard, 1976.
The Song of the Sea Otter by Edith T. Hurd. Pantheon, 1983.

Index

Picture Acknowledgments

The photographs in this book were supplied by: Bruce Coleman Ltd: D. & J. Bartlett 25, R. & M. Borland 11, M.N. Boulton 40, J. Burton 30, 33 (right), F. Erize 22, J. Foote 29, 31 (right), 36, 39 (left), P.A. Hinchliffe 17 (right), H. Jungius 9, G. Langsbury 10, M.T. O'Keefe 26, H. Reinhard 33 (left), L. Rue Jr. 28, B. Tulloch 21; Frank Lane Picture Agency: M. Clark 8, D. Dugan 43 (left), M. Hamblin 37, J. Hosking 17 (left), F.W. Lane 16, S. Maslowski 12, W. Rohdich 15 (right), 23, 24, 42, L.L. Rue 43 (right), Silvestris 31 (left); Oxford Scientific Films: J. Dermid 14, 18 (right), T. Levin (Animals Animals) 27 (right), Stouffer Productions Inc. 27 (left) 38; Planet Earth Pictures: J. Camenzind *frontispiece*, J. Scott 11; South American Pictures: T. Morrison 18 (left), 39 (right); Survival Anglia: J. Foott 15 (left), 23, 32, 34, B. Wheeler *cover*. The illustrations on pages 13, 19, 35 and 41 were supplied by Wendy Meadway.